Countries Around the World

Iceland

Melanie Waldron

Heinemann Library
Chicago, Illinois

www.capstonepub.com
Visit our website to find out more information about Heinemann-Raintree books.

To order:

☎ Phone 888-454-2279

💻 Visit www.capstonepub.com to browse our catalog and order online.

Edited by Laura Knowles
Designed by Victoria Allen
Original illustrations © Capstone Global Library Ltd 2012
Illustrated by Oxford Designers and Illustrators
Picture research by Mica Brancic
Originated by Capstone Global Library Ltd
Printed and bound in China by CTPS

15 14 13 12 11
10 9 8 7 6 5 4 3 2 1

Library of Congress Cataloging-in-Publication Data
Waldron, Melanie.
   Iceland / Melanie Waldron.
      p. cm.—(Countries around the world)
   Includes bibliographical references and index.
   ISBN 978-1-4329-6099-5 (hbk.)—ISBN 978-1-4329-6125-1
(pbk.) 1. Iceland—Juvenile literature. I. Title.
   DL305.W35 2012
   949.12—dc22   2011015419

5040   7385   0/13 (handwritten)

Acknowledgments
We would like to thank the following for permission to reproduce photographs: Alamy pp. **9** (© Bjarki Reyr REK), **25** (© Bjarki Reyr FCR), **28** (© Jeremy Hoare); Corbis pp. **5** (© Julian Calverley), **7** (© Atlantide Phototravel/Guido Cozzi), **11** (© Arctic-Images), **17** (© Wilfried Krecichwost), **22** (epa/ © Justin Lane), **30** (© Imaginechina); iStockphoto pp. **13** (© Subtik), **27** (© hughalison), **32** (© Dan Booth), Shutterstock pp. **15** (© Tomasz Parys), **18** (© Arnold van Wijk - Landscape Photographer), **19** (© Arto Hakola), **20** (© Tatonka), **21** (© Ventura), **29** (© Petur Asgeirsson), **33** (© ElenaGaak), **35** (© Renewer), **39** (© David Brynjar Sigurjonsson), **46** (© Christophe Testi).

Cover photograph of a group of climbers on the Vatnajokull Glacier, Iceland, reproduced with permission of Photolibrary/ Ingram Publishing RF.

We would like to thank Daniel Block for his invaluable help in the preparation of this book.

Every effort has been made to contact copyright holders of material reproduced in this book. Any omissions will be rectified in subsequent printings if notice is given to the publisher.

Contents

Some words are printed in bold, **like this**. You can find out what they mean by looking in the glossary.

Introducing Iceland

In early 2010, Iceland was being watched by people all over the world. Many airplanes could not fly because of an enormous cloud of ash that was covering the skies over northwest Europe. The ash was coming from a volcano in Iceland called Eyjafjallajökull, which was erupting. Aircraft engineers were worried that this ash could clog airplane engines and cause them to crash. The eruption eventually stopped in May 2010, and flights resumed as normal.

You may have heard about the ash cloud and Iceland. What else do you know about the country? Its name suggests a cold, **barren** country, covered in snow and ice. But there is so much more to Iceland.

Land of fire and ice

Iceland is often called "the land of fire and ice." Much of the country is covered by huge **ice caps** and **glaciers**, but these frozen areas are dotted with volcanoes. Many of these are active. Along the coast there are many **fjords** and little islands. Most people live around the coastal areas.

Iceland is an island in northwest Europe, located in the northern part of the Atlantic Ocean. The United Kingdom and Norway are to the south and east, and Greenland and Canada are to the west. Iceland is slightly smaller than the state of Kentucky and has a very small population of just over 300,000 people. It is a beautiful island, with amazing scenery and some vast empty spaces. Icelanders live a very modern and **cosmopolitan** life. There is much more to Iceland than just fire and ice!

How to say...

hello	*halló*	(HAL-low)	**yes**	*já*	(yow)
goodbye	*bless*	(bless)	**no**	*nei*	(nay)
I'm from	*ég er frá*	(yeg air frow)	**thank you**	*takk fyrir*	(TAC FEAR-ir)
my name is	*ég heiti*	(yeg HAY-it)			

In April 2010, the Eyjafjallajökull volcano in Iceland started erupting. It spewed millions of tons of ash into the atmosphere.

History: A Young Country

Iceland's position, just below the Arctic Circle and in the middle of the Atlantic Ocean, meant that early explorers did not know it existed. It was simply too far north and too far away. The Greek explorer Pytheas may have been the first to write about an island far to the north of Britain, in 330 BCE. The first regular visitors to Iceland were most likely Irish monks in the 700s CE. They traveled there looking for a quiet, uninhabited place where they could devote themselves to prayer.

The first **settlers** to arrive and stay in Iceland were **Vikings** from Norway and Sweden. They started coming from around 850 CE. They traveled across the ocean in open boats with all their belongings, including their farm animals! In order to decide where to land on the island, one settler, named Ingólfur Arnarson, followed an old custom. He threw the wooden pillars of his chieftain's seat into the sea, just off the coast of Iceland. He followed these pillars along the coast to see where the sea washed them up, and that is where he settled. He called this place Reykjavík. Today, it is Iceland's capital city.

The world's oldest parliament

By 930 CE Iceland's settlers decided that they needed some kind of government. The island's chieftains gathered to create the **Althing**, now recognized as the world's oldest **parliament**. The Althing met for two weeks every year at a place called Thingvellir in southwest Iceland.

In 1000 CE the Althing met to settle the issue of religion. There had been disputes between **pagans** and Christians, and the Althing eventually decided to convert Iceland to full Christianity.

The long ridge of rock at Thingvellir was where speakers would stand to address the Althing.

The Sturlung Age

From the late 1100s, Icelandic society started deteriorating. There was fighting between rival chieftains, and farms and homes were raided. By 1220, six wealthy families ruled the whole island, and by 1262 they had all agreed to be ruled by the king of Norway. This time of upheaval was known as the Sturlung Age, after the largest wealthy family, the Sturlungs. Although the Althing still existed under Norway's rule, it had very limited power. In 1397, control of Iceland then passed to Denmark after Norway, Sweden, and Denmark united.

As well as suffering from political upheaval, Icelanders also suffered from natural disasters during this time. Cold, hard winters killed many crops and animals, and volcanic eruptions covered a third of the island in ash. The **Black Death** arrived in Iceland in 1402, and in less than two years it wiped out half of Iceland's population.

How to say...

rule	*regla*	(REG-la)
independence	*sjálfstæði*	(SYALV-sty-thi)
farm	*bæ*	(BYE-r)
winter	*vetur*	(V-etur)
eruption	*gos*	(GO-os)
import	*innflutningur*	(INN-flutningur)
export	*útflutningur*	(OOT-flutningur)

Return to independence

By the 1800s, many Icelanders were demanding **independence**. At the same time, towns were growing bigger and people were **importing** modern farm equipment and wood for boats. They were also **exporting** livestock, wool, and fish. In 1918, Iceland signed the Act of Union, which made the country an independent state within Denmark. When Denmark was occupied by Germany during World War II, Iceland took the chance to take control of itself again. Finally, on June 17, 1944, Iceland became completely independent.

Icelanders celebrate Independence Day every year on June 17.

20th-century Iceland

Iceland has never had a strong military force. During World War II, therefore, U.S. troops were based at Keflavík in southwest Iceland, leaving in 1946. Iceland joined **NATO** in 1949, and the United States returned in 1951, when the threat of war with the **USSR** seemed a possibility. U.S. forces stayed there until 2006, when the military base was finally closed.

After World War II, Iceland saw a lot of development. The main road around Iceland (the Ring Road) was completed in 1974, and power stations were built. The fishing industry grew, and Iceland exported fish to many European countries. This brought a lot of money into the country, and much of it was spent on modernizing Iceland. The huge expansion of the fishing industry also led to the "cod wars" with the United Kingdom. Iceland's **trawlers** were sailing further and further from the Icelandic coast to find fish. The United Kingdom disagreed with this because it wanted to fish in that part of the sea, too. The British Navy sent ships to protect British trawlers from the Icelandic coastguard boats, which were cutting their nets. In 1976 both countries agreed on fishing areas, and the "cod wars" ended.

Daily life

Need to find a phone number? Icelandic telephone directories list people by their first names. Names are made up of a first or given name, followed by the father's (or, sometimes, mother's) name. If you are a boy, you will have "son" on the end of your father's name, and if you are a girl you will have "dottir." Here are some examples:

Erik Magnusson	(Erik, son of Magnus)
Svana Magnusdottir	(Svana, daughter of Magnus)
Hanna Hinrikdottir	(Hanna, daughter of Hinrik)
Ari Hinrikson	(Ari, son of Hinrik)

Fishing is still a huge part of the Icelandic economy. Cod is one of the main catches in the Atlantic Ocean.

An economic crisis

In September 2008, the global economic crisis hit Iceland, whose banks had big investments in other countries. This meant that when the global crisis hit, the small Icelandic **economy** was badly affected. Banks collapsed, many people lost their jobs, and others had their wages cut. To help the situation, Iceland applied for **European Union (EU)** membership in July 2009, but it can take years for membership to be finalized. Many economists feel that changing the currency from the Icelandic króna to the **euro** will help the economy to recover.

Regions and Resources: Landscape and Economy

Iceland has a large central **plateau** surrounded by low-lying land at the coast. Around half of the island is more than 1,300 feet (400 meters) above sea level. The south coast is dominated by a huge black sand **plain**. Around the east, north, and northwest coasts there are **fjords** and sea cliffs. The southwest has flatter coastal areas and is where most of the population lives.

There are large ice fields and **glaciers** in Iceland—15 percent of the country is covered in ice! The low-lying land around the coast is fertile and used for farming, while much of the central plateau is bare rock.

This map shows Iceland's main physical features.

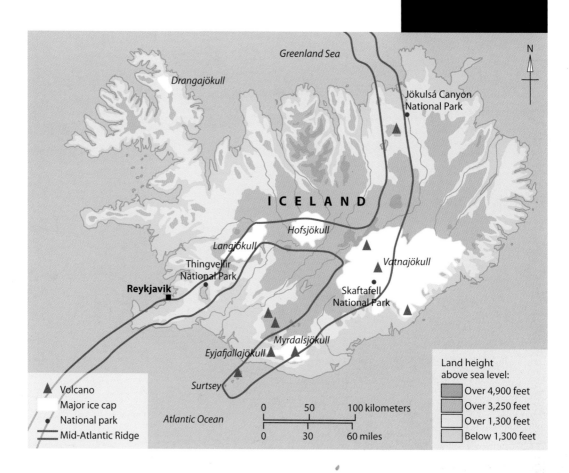

Greenland Sea

Drangajökull

Jökulsá Canyon National Park

ICELAND

Hofsjökull

Langjökull

Thingvellir National Park

Reykjavik

Vatnajökull

Skaftafell National Park

Myrdalsjökull

Eyjafjallajökull

Surtsey

Atlantic Ocean

N

▲	Volcano
	Major ice cap
•	National park
=	Mid-Atlantic Ridge

0	50	100 kilometers
0	30	60 miles

Land height above sea level:
- Over 4,900 feet
- Over 3,250 feet
- Over 1,300 feet
- Below 1,300 feet

Tectonic Iceland

Iceland sits on the Mid-Atlantic Ridge, where two plates of Earth's crust meet and where new crust is created. Volcanoes lie all along the ridge, and there are many of these in Iceland. Twenty-two of them are active, and this means that, in places, Iceland's landscape changes frequently. To the south of the main island lie the Westman Islands, all created by erupting volcanoes. The youngest island is Surtsey. It was created in 1963, when an underwater volcano erupted and threw out so much lava that a new island was born.

The Northern Lights

On cold, clear nights in Iceland, and with a bit of luck, you might catch a glimpse of the Northern Lights, also called the Aurora Borealis. These are amazing sheets of red and green light in the night sky, caused by charged particles in Earth's atmosphere.

The Aurora Borealis, or Northern Lights, is a beautiful spectacle.

Cold water, hot water

There are some enormous **ice caps** in Iceland. The largest is Vatnajökull, which measures 3,200 square miles (8,300 square kilometers)—this is larger than every other ice cap and glacier in Iceland and Europe combined! Melting water from the ice caps and glaciers contribute to the numerous rivers that flow through Iceland. Many of these rivers are incredibly impressive as they have carved deep canyons through the hard rock. There are also some amazing waterfalls, for example Gullfoss in the southwest of Iceland.

Where water is heated by the hot volcanic crust, hot springs can be found. There are about 800 hot springs in Iceland, and many are almost boiling hot. Some of these hot springs erupt to form **geysers**, shooting boiling water up into the sky. One of the most exciting is called Strokkur.

YOUNG PEOPLE

After school, many of Reykjavìk's teenagers head to the **thermal pool** at Árbæjarlaug. It has outdoor and indoor pools, water slides and fountains, three "hot pots," steam baths, and saunas. The outdoor pool is especially popular in winter, even when it is snowing!

An Arctic climate?

Although Iceland lies just below the Arctic Circle, the climate is not as cold as you might expect. This is because of the warm sea currents in the Atlantic Ocean. Average Reykjavík winter temperatures are 28 to 36 degrees Fahrenheit, and in summer are 48 to 57 degrees Fahrenheit. There is plenty of rain and snow.

One remarkable thing about Iceland is the amount of daylight it gets. In winter there are only around four hours of daylight, while in the summer the sun only sets for around three hours.

Around every six minutes, Strokkur geyser shoots boiling water about 50 to 100 feet (15 to 30 meters) into the sky!

Iceland's resources

The sea around Iceland provides one of the country's major resources—fish. The fishing industry is huge, and 40 percent of Iceland's **exports** are related to the fishing industry. The fish—mostly prawns, cod, haddock, and herring—are sold mainly to the United States, Europe, and Japan. The farmland in Iceland is mostly used to produce meat and dairy products for the people of Iceland. Very little is exported. Other main products are potatoes and other vegetables.

Iceland's position on the Mid-Atlantic Ridge provides the country with a very valuable resource—power. As well as **hydroelectric power**, Iceland has **geothermal power**. This is where Earth's hot crust heats water, which is then used to heat buildings and to create steam. This steam is used to create clean electricity, with no pollution produced as a result. Many industries that use a lot of energy have been set up in Iceland to take advantage of this cheap, green electricity. One example of this is **aluminum smelting**.

This map shows the locations of Iceland's main geothermal power plants and aluminum smelters.

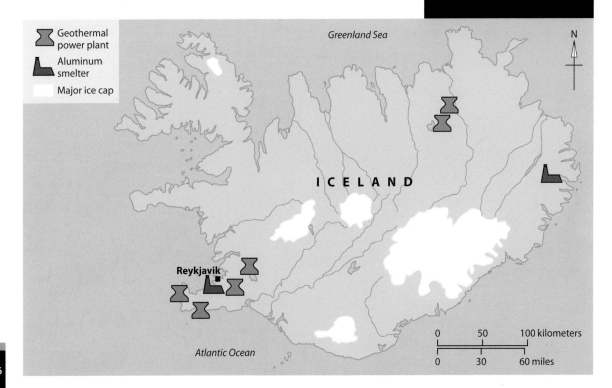

The power stations and industrial factories, however, do have an impact on the landscape. Many Icelanders are concerned about this and would prefer more investment in other industries, for example IT, **biotechnology**, finance and **service industries**. Tourism is very important to Iceland, and in 2006 the number of visitors to Iceland was larger than Iceland's population!

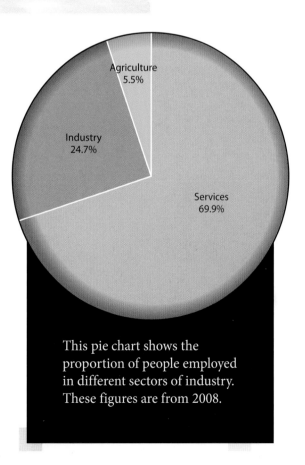

Agriculture
5.5%

Industry
24.7%

Services
69.9%

This pie chart shows the proportion of people employed in different sectors of industry. These figures are from 2008.

Wildlife: A Pristine Environment

At first glance, Iceland's large areas of exposed rock, ice, and lava fields may not seem to contain much wildlife. However, there is an amazing range of plants and animals to be found—you just have to look closely! Iceland has three national parks and more than 80 reserves, parks, and monuments.

Land mammals

The Arctic fox is Iceland's only **native** mammal. Its coat turns white in winter to provide camouflage as it hunts for its prey. Reindeer were brought over from Norway and now run wild in the eastern part of the island. Icelandic horses are descended from horses brought by early **settlers**. No other horses were allowed into the country after 982 CE, so the Icelandic horse breed has remained pure.

Icelandic horses are strong and hardy. They cope well with Iceland's long and cold winters.

Bird life

You do not have to search hard to find birds in Iceland. During the summer months you can see huge colonies of sea birds, such as gannets, guillemots, and puffins. Many migrating birds stop off in Iceland throughout the year.

The Arctic tern is one of Iceland's most interesting birds. These birds **migrate** from Antarctica, more than 19,000 miles (32,000 kilometers) away. They come to Iceland to breed, but they make their nests on stony fields. Anyone walking near a nest is likely to come under attack! The birds will dive-bomb anything they see as a threat. One way to avoid a nasty cut on the head is to carry a stick above your head—the birds always aim for the highest part of the threat.

Here, an Arctic tern is feeding her chick.

How to say...

wildlife	*dýralíf*	(DEERA-leaf)
horse	*hestur*	(HES-tur)
bird	*fugl*	(FOO-gl)
fox	*refur*	(REV-ur)
reindeer	*hreindýr*	(HRAYN-deer)
puffin	*lundi*	(LOON-di)

Marine life

The rich waters around Iceland's coast provide excellent feeding grounds for marine life. Many species of whale can be found, including narwhals and beluga whales. The blue whale, the largest animal on Earth, is a common sight. Dolphins, porpoises, and seals are also often spotted around the coast.

Iceland is one of the world's best places to go whale-watching, and many tourists are drawn to the country because of this.

Plant life

There are very few forests remaining on Iceland. Most were cut down by the early settlers to provide timber for building houses and ships and to clear land for grazing animals. The small pockets of forest that remain are mainly dwarf birch and willow forest. Moss and **lichen** cover much of Iceland. They are very well adapted to the cold winters and strong winds. In summer, more than 440 species of flowering plant create a beautiful sight on the island.

Environmental issues

High winds and **overgrazing** have caused a lot of soil **erosion**. In some places the erosion has been so dramatic that only bare rock remains. One solution was planting the non-native lupin, a plant that binds the soil together with its roots. However, the lupin also spreads quickly and is in danger of pushing out Iceland's native plants.

Whale hunting is an issue that divides Iceland. While most of the world calls for whale hunting to be banned, some Icelanders feel that it is part of their national **identity**. Others argue that the money raised from tourists coming simply to watch whales is worth far more to the country.

Another issue that splits Icelanders is whether more power stations should be built. Although these have an impact on the landscape, the power created is pollution-free. In general, because Iceland has a small population, large areas of wilderness, little heavy industry, and "green" power reserves, the environment is almost completely unspoiled.

Purple-blue lupins help to protect soil from erosion, but they grow quickly and push out other plants.

Infrastructure: Running the Country

A country's infrastructure is the set of systems and services that are needed for everyday life to run properly. The infrastructure includes power and water supplies, transportation and communication systems, schools, and hospitals. The Icelandic government runs the country and makes sure everything works smoothly.

There are five main political parties in Iceland. Elections to the **Althing** are held at least every four years, and there are 63 members of the Althing. Women were granted the right to vote in 1915, just ahead of the United Kingdom in 1918 and the United States in 1920. The first female member of the Althing was elected in 1922. During the 2009 elections, 27 women were elected, making up 43 percent of the Althing.

JÓHANNA SIGURÐARDÓTTIR
(BORN 1942)

Jóhanna Sigurðardóttir, leader of the Social Democratic Alliance, became Iceland's first female prime minister in February 2009. She was born in Reykjavík in 1942 and worked for nine years as a flight attendant. She was first elected to the Althing in 1978. She has been a strong supporter of rights for handicapped, elderly, and disadvantaged people, and this has earned her the nickname "Saint Johanna."

The president

Iceland also has a president, elected every four years. The current president is Ólafur Ragnar Grímsson, who was first elected in 1996, and re-elected in 2000, 2004, and 2008. Before him the president was Vigdís Finnbogadóttir, the first woman in the world to be elected as president. She served from 1980 until 1996, when she stood down. The president is the **head of state**, and the government must have the president's agreement on new laws.

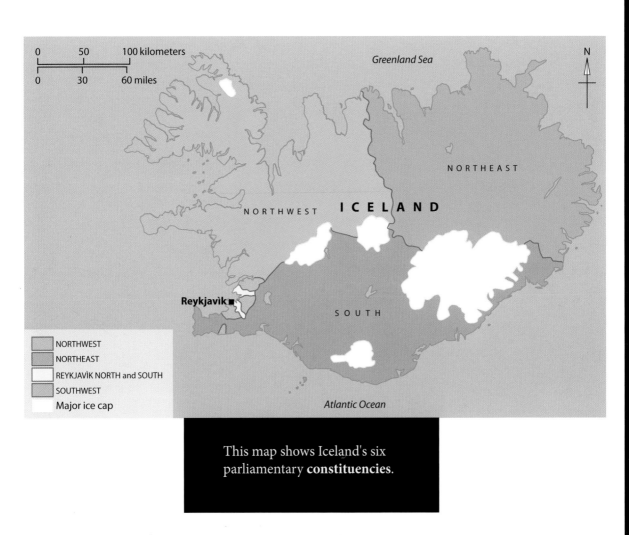

This map shows Iceland's six parliamentary **constituencies**.

Schools in Iceland

Most Icelandic children will attend some form of preschool (*leikskóli*) until they are six years old. From six to sixteen, education is **compulsory**. Primary and lower secondary education (*grunnskóli*) usually takes place in the same school. Upper secondary education (*framhaldsskóli*) is not compulsory, and students are usually ages 16 to 20.

The *grunnskóli* school year lasts nine months, from around early September to early June. Lessons take place five days a week. The size of schools can vary—in Reykjavík some schools have around 800 pupils, while some rural schools have only 10 pupils.

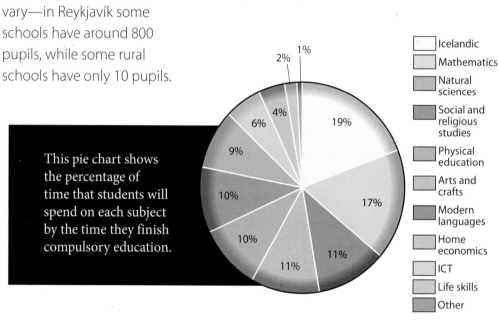

This pie chart shows the percentage of time that students will spend on each subject by the time they finish compulsory education.

Legend: Icelandic, Mathematics, Natural sciences, Social and religious studies, Physical education, Arts and crafts, Modern languages, Home economics, ICT, Life skills, Other

Daily life

There is no school uniform in Iceland. A typical school day begins at 8:10 a.m. and ends at 1:50 p.m. Most schools offer a hot meal at lunchtime, for example a pasta dish or soup. Most children walk to school, although in rural areas many travel by car or bus. From the age of six, most children will attend after-school clubs or do sports, for example soccer (what they call football), handball, figure skating, ice hockey, basketball, or swimming.

These students in Reykjavík are playing soccer on a cold October morning.

School holidays

During their summer vacation, most children living in cities used to go and spend some time helping on farms. However, this is becoming much less common, as most work on farms is now done by machine. In place of this, many children will travel abroad with their families during the summer, usually to the United States or Europe. Many families also own homes in the countryside and spend weekends and holidays there.

Health care in Iceland

Iceland's level of health care is considered to be very high. It is mostly funded by the **taxes** that people pay to the government. Because of good health care and the high standard of living in general, life expectancy is among the highest in the world. Life expectancy for men is 79.6 years and for women is 83 years. This ranks Iceland at 17th compared to other countries in the world. The United States is ranked 49th, and the United Kingdom is ranked 28th.

Iceland's health issues are similar to many other developed countries. High standards of living mean that **obesity** rates are quite high, although not as high as the United States. Levels of smoking are lower than in the United States and United Kingdom. In all three countries, cancer is one of the biggest causes of death.

Travel in Iceland

The road network in Iceland is small. There are very few roads crossing the vast uninhabited areas. The Ring Road circles the country and is the main road connecting most towns and villages. The roads branching off the Ring Road are often made of gravel, and many cross through—not over—rivers! This means that a four-wheel-drive vehicle is essential in many areas.

Flying is often the best way to travel around, and there are many domestic airports. It can sometimes be cheaper than taking the bus. Ferries provide a good service to and from settlements on the rugged coastlines in the northwest. Iceland has no public railway system.

Where do Icelanders live?

Because Iceland's interior is largely uninhabitable, most settlements are located around the coast. Many of the coastal towns and villages sprang up when the fishing industry boomed in the 20th century. However, with modern **trawlers** requiring far fewer workers, many villagers are moving to the capital city, Reykjavík, to find work.

Many of Iceland's roads cross through rivers. Some vehicles are fitted with "snorkels" so that the engine does not cut out due to lack of air when the vehicle goes through the water.

Culture: Language, Literature, and Leisure

Iceland's **culture** is strong and distinct—it is unlike any other culture. This is because of its small population and its isolated position in the Atlantic Ocean. Family ties and communities are strong, and living standards are high. Because of this, crime rates are very low. Most of the population—94 percent—are descended from the original settlers. The rest are foreign **immigrants**, mostly from Europe.

A strong language

The Icelandic language is related to Scandinavian languages such as Danish, Norwegian, and Swedish. Iceland is very protective of its language. An Iceland Language Council discusses which new words need to be added to the language. This prevents new words from other languages, such as English, from entering into it.

Daily life

Until 1988 there was only one television station in Iceland, and it did not broadcast on Thursdays! Now there are four stations, showing a mix of Icelandic, British, and American programs (with subtitles if necessary). The children's program *Lazytown*—starring Stephanie, Sportacus, and Robbie Rotten—is made in Iceland.

Almost everyone in Iceland enjoys taking a dip in one of the country's numerous pools, which are all heated naturally.

Sports

Soccer (what they call football) is very popular in Iceland—both playing it and supporting a particular team. Many people also play handball. This is a bit like basketball, but the goal is like a small football net rather than a hooped basketball net. Iceland won the silver medal in handball at the 2008 Olympic Games in Beijing, China.

A traditional Icelandic sport is *glíma* (wrestling), which dates back to the 9th century. Some people still take part, and you can see *glíma* demonstrations at certain festivals. The most popular sport—and social activity—is swimming. Swimming pools are found in almost every town and village, heated by **geothermal** energy.

Handball is an exciting and popular sport across Iceland.

Literature—the sagas

It is part of Icelandic culture to read and write, and the **literacy rate** is an amazing 99.9 percent. This love of literature dates back to the 12th and 13th centuries, when the Icelandic sagas were written. These are long, complex stories about families, history, war, travel, romance, and adventure. They were kept alive through the centuries as people gathered in the evenings to hear them, and today they are still told and loved.

Halldór Laxness is one of Iceland's most famous modern authors. He won the Nobel Prize for literature in 1955. Arnaldur Indridason, who writes books about crime in Rekjavik, is one of today's most popular Icelandic authors.

Music

Many traditional Icelandic songs are based on the sagas. Most were simply sung, with no instruments played to accompany them. There are two favorite traditional songs that are still learned today. One is a cowboy song about sheep herders and outlaws, and the other is a lullaby about an outlaw's wife who threw her starving baby into a waterfall!

Pop music is a hobby for many Icelanders. A lot of people form bands and play in small venues, especially in Reykjavík. The Airwaves festival, held in Reykjavík in October, shows off Iceland's best local talent. Famous international bands also play there.

BJÖRK (BORN 1965)

Born in Reykjavík, Björk Gudmundsdóttir is perhaps Iceland's best known pop star. She recorded her first album when she was only 12 and bought a piano with the money she made from selling it. She went on to sing in a band called The Sugarcubes, which became popular in Europe and the United States. Björk then went solo, and she has made a very successful career for herself.

Björk is known for her distinctive costumes and makeup, as well as for her music.

Religion and the supernatural

The largest religion in Iceland is the Christian Lutheran religion—more than 80 percent of the population belong to this church. Although less than 10 percent of the population regularly attend church, almost every Icelander will attend at least once a year. This is because the Lutheran religion is seen as part of the Icelandic national **identity**. There are small churches all over the island, and many churches also hold social events such as plays, poetry readings, and concerts.

Many Icelanders believe in mysterious spirits or *huldufólk* (hidden people). They are thought to live in the lava fields and rocky outcrops around the island. There are stories of these *huldufólk* **jinxing** construction projects—machinery breaks down, workers become ill, or the weather halts work. The jinxes only stop when the road or building is relocated away from the *huldufólk* land.

This church in northern Iceland has a roof made from **turf**. This type of building was common in Iceland for around 1,000 years.

Food

Fish and seafood are an important part of Icelandic cuisine. Lamb is also very common. Traditional Icelandic cooking did not waste anything, but today meals like *svið* (sheep's head) and *hákarl* (rotten shark meat) are rarely seen! Beef, horse, and reindeer meat appear on some menus, as well as puffin and guillemot (types of seabird).

Skyr is a traditional dairy food, a bit like yogurt, which is still very popular in Iceland. Other sweet treats include pancakes and doughnuts. Icelandic people love coffee and drink more Coca-Cola per person than any other country! You can buy bottled water, but the tap water is pure, free, and delicious.

Bláberjaskyrterta (blueberry skyr torte)

Ask an adult to help you make this delicious Icelandic dessert.

Ingredients

- 9 ounces graham crackers (about 18 crackers)
- 3½ tablespoons butter
- 9 ounces plain *skyr* (yogurt)
- 9 ounces vanilla *skyr* (yogurt)
- 16 ounces whipping cream
- 9 ounces blueberries

What to do

1. Crunch up the graham crackers, melt the butter, and mix together. Press the mixture into the bottom of a 9-inch-diameter cake pan.
2. Whip the cream until it forms peaks, and carefully mix in the two types of *skyr* (yogurt). Spoon this over the graham cracker mixture.
3. Sprinkle the blueberries on top, and refrigerate for two hours before serving.

Iceland Today

Iceland hit the world headlines in 2010 because of the Eyjafjallajökull eruption ash cloud. The previous year, Iceland had also been in the news because of the global economic crash. The financial problems have caused unemployment to rise, wages to be cut, and standards of living to drop slightly. However, Icelanders are hard-working and **patriotic** people, and they are working hard to recover from the crash.

Much to celebrate

Despite the recent problems facing Iceland's **economy**, the country still has a lot to be proud of:

- Icelandic society is very fair, and there is more equality between men and women than in any other country.

- The excellent education and health care systems mean that everyone is given the best chances in life.

- The clean, "green" energy supply from the vast reserves of geothermal energy will become increasingly valuable in our modern world.

- Iceland is very technologically advanced, with high levels of Internet access (84 percent) and a higher number of mobile phones than people.

- The landscape is truly amazing and is unlikely to be lost through mass development.

- There is a huge range of outdoor activities to offer everyone, including bird-watching, caving, cycling, diving, hiking, horse riding, kayaking, skiing, and whale-watching.

Although the Eyjafjallajökull eruption caused chaos and kept tourists away, now that the eruption has ended it is actually attracting more tourists to Iceland. People want to see how the landscape has changed since the eruption and to find out what else Iceland has to offer. This is another sign that Iceland's future looks good.

Reykjavík and the rest of Iceland are beginning to bounce back after the economic crisis of 2008.

Fact File

Official name:	Iceland
Official language:	Icelandic
Capital city:	Reykjavík
Type of government:	constitutional republic
Currency:	Icelandic króna
Bordering countries:	none
Land area:	39,770 square miles (103,000 square kilometers)
Population:	308,910 people (2010 estimate)
Largest cities and populations:	Reykjavík (117,505 people) Kópavogur (30,357 people) Hafnarfjörður (25,913 people) Akureyri (17,295 people)
Birth rate:	13.36 births per 1,000 people
Death rate:	6.9 deaths per 1,000 people
Life expectancy:	79.6 years for men; 83 years for women
Ethnic groups:	Icelandic 94 percent; other 6 percent
Unemployment rate:	8.2 percent
Literacy rate:	99 percent of the population can read and write
Number of mobile phones:	342,000 (more than the population!)
Climate:	temperate; moderated by North Atlantic current; mild, windy winters; damp, cool summers
Highest point:	Hvannadalshnukur (at Vatnajökull glacier) 6,923 feet (2,110 meters)
Coastline length:	3,088 miles (4,970 kilometers)
Natural hazards:	earthquakes and volcanic activity

Major rivers:	Thjórsá, Jökulsá á Fjöllum
Deepest lake:	Lake Öskjuvatn—712 feet (217 meters) deep
Largest lake:	Thingvallavatn—32 square miles (84 square kilometers)
Biggest waterfalls:	Skógafoss—197 feet (60 meters) high Dettifoss—144 feet (44 meters) high Gullfoss—105 feet (32 meters) high
Natural resources:	fish, hydroelectric power, geothermal power
Major industries:	fish processing, aluminum smelting, geothermal power, hydroelectric power, tourism
Imports:	machinery and equipment, petroleum products, foodstuffs, textiles
Exports:	fish and fish products (40 percent), aluminum, animal products, ferrosilicon, diatomite

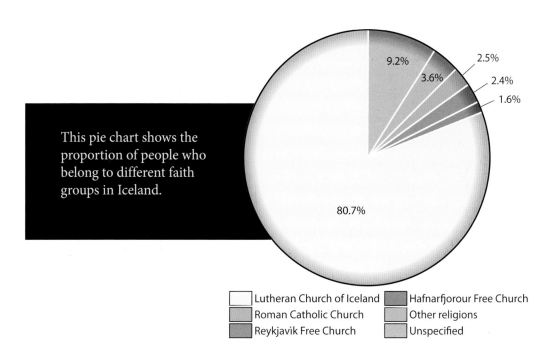

This pie chart shows the proportion of people who belong to different faith groups in Iceland.

9.2% 3.6% 2.5% 2.4% 1.6% 80.7%

- Lutheran Church of Iceland
- Roman Catholic Church
- Reykjavík Free Church
- Hafnarfjorour Free Church
- Other religions
- Unspecified

National anthem:	*Ó Guð vors lands* (O, God of Our Land)
National plant:	Mountain Avens
Famous Icelanders:	Leif Eriksson (explorer, around 1000s), Halldór Laxness (Nobel prize-winning novelist, 1902–1998), Magnus Magnusson (writer and TV presenter, 1929–2007), Jóhanna Sigurðardottir (current prime minister, born 1942), Björk Gudmundsdottir (singer-songwriter, born 1965), Hermann Hreiðarsson (soccer player, born 1974).
Public holidays:	New Year's Day (January 1), Easter (Holy Thursday, Good Friday, Easter Monday), First day of summer (First Thursday after April 18), Labor Day (May 1), Ascension Day (May or June), Whit Sunday and Whit Monday (May or June), Independence Day (June 17), Shop and Office Workers' Holiday (First Monday in August), Christmas (December 24 to 26), New Year's Eve (December 31).

The Vatnajokull glacier is just one of the spectacular features of Iceland's landscape.

Timeline

BCE means "before the common era." When this appears after a date it refers to the number of years before the Christian religion began. BCE dates are always counted backward.

CE means "common era." When this appears after a date, it refers to the time after the Christian religion began.

700 CE	Irish monks start visiting Iceland
850 CE	**Viking settlers** from Norway and Sweden arrive
871 CE	A Viking from Norway, Ingólfur Arnarson, names his settlement Reykjavík (which means "Smoky Bay")
930 CE	The **Althing** is created
982 CE	A ban on bringing horses to Iceland begins
1000	Iceland fully converts to Christianity
1100s–1200s	Icelandic society breaks down as tribes fight
1262	Iceland is ruled by the king of Norway
1300	The volcano Hekla erupts, causing many deaths
1341	Hekla erupts again, causing more deaths and starvation
1389	Hekla erupts yet again
1397	Denmark rules Iceland
1402–1404	The **Black Death** wipes out half the population
1550	The Protestant Lutheran religion spreads across Iceland
1627	Pirates raid the east coast of Iceland, taking hundreds of prisoners
1783–1784	The volcano Laki erupts, killing 25 percent of the population and 50 percent of farm animals

1800s	Many Icelanders start demanding **independence**
1915	Women are given the right to vote
1918	Iceland signs the Act of Union, becoming an independent state within Denmark
1922	The first woman is elected to the Althing
1944	Iceland becomes fully independent
1946	U.S. troops leave their base at Keflavík
1949	Iceland joins **NATO**
1951	U.S. troops return to Keflavík
1963	The island of Surtsey is created by a volcano
1974	The Ring Road around the island is completed
1976	Iceland and the United Kingdom finally agree on fishing-ground boundaries
1980	Iceland elects the first female president in the world
2006	U.S. troops finally leave Iceland, and the base at Keflavík is closed
2008	Iceland's **economy** crashes
2009	Iceland applies for EU membership
2010	Eruption of Eyjafjallajökull volcano

Glossary

Althing Icelandic parliament (like Congress)

aluminum smelting extracting the metal aluminum from its raw material, aluminum oxide

barren infertile, not able to grow crops

biotechnology science that uses very small living things to make things such as medicine

Black Death deadly plague (disease), which often showed as dark patches on the skin

compulsory necessary, required or demanded

constituency area or district where a member of parliament is elected by the people living there

cosmopolitan having influences from all over the world

culture practices, traditions, and beliefs of a society

economy relating to the money, industry, and jobs in a country

euro official currency of 12 European Union nations

erosion wearing away of Earth's surface by wind, water, and ice

European Union (EU) organization of European countries with shared political and economic aims. The EU formed from the EEC (European Economic Community) in 1993.

export sell goods to another country. The goods are also referred to as "exports."

fjord long, narrow ocean inlet that passes between high and rocky banks or steep cliffs

geothermal power electricity generated from the heat inside Earth

geyser spring that shoots a stream of hot water, steam, or mud into the air

glacier large mass of ice formed very slowly in cold regions from compacted snow moving down a slope or across land

head of state main public representative of a country, such as a queen or president

hydroelectric power electricity generated by moving water

identity characteristics by which someone or something is known

ice cap thick layer of ice that covers a large area of land all year round

immigrant person who has moved to another country and settled there

import buy goods from another country. The goods are also referred to as "imports."

independence having freedom from outside control

jinx cause someone or something to have bad luck

lichen living organism that is made of a fungus that lives together with algae or bacteria

literacy rate proportion of people who are able to read

migrate change habitat or location, usually when the seasons change

native relating to an animal or plant that is found naturally in a certain place

NATO stands for North Atlantic Treaty Organization. A group of mainly Western nations that have promised to defend each other in times of need.

obese very overweight. A person suffering from obesity is very overweight.

overgrazing when animals strip too much vegetation from the land's surface, leaving the soil and rock exposed

pagan someone who practiced a religion where many different things are worshipped. Usually, "pagan" refers to the religion practiced before conversion to Christianity.

parliament group of people who make laws for a country, similar to Congress

patriotic feeling or showing love for, and loyalty to, your country

plain low-lying area of flat land

plateau large, flat area of high land

service industries jobs that are involved with providing knowledge and time to help others

settler person who settles in a new area

tax money paid by people to the government. Taxes can come from wages or be placed on goods that people buy.

thermal pool pool of water heated by Earth's crust

trawler fishing boat that hauls a net

turf top layer of soil with grass

USSR stands for Union of Soviet Socialist Republics, also called the Soviet Union. The USSR was an empire in which communist Russia controlled neighboring countries from 1917 to 1991.

Viking sea warrior or trader from Scandinavia

Find Out More

Books

Deady, Kathleen W. *Iceland*. Danbury, CT: Children's Press, 2005.

Fradin, Judith and Dennis Fradin. *Volcano!: The Icelandic Eruption of 2010 and Other Hot, Smoky, Fierce, and Fiery Mountians*. Washington, DC: National Geographic Children's Books, 2010.

Hapka, Catherine. *Elska* (Horse Diaries). New York: Random House, 2009.

Miller, Jennifer A. *Iceland*. Minneapolis, MN: Lerner Publishing Group, 2010.

Sheen, Barbara. *Foods of Iceland*. San Diego, CA: Kidhaven Press, 2011.

Wilcox, Jonathan and Zawiah Abdul Latif. *Iceland, 2nd Edition*. New York: Benchmark Books, 2007.

DVDs

Nature Wonders series (icluding several titles on different destinations in Iceland). Tampa, FL: TravelVideoStore.com, 2008.

Ian Wright. *Globe Trekker: Iceland & Greenland*. Directed by Ian Cross. Los Angeles, CA: 555 Productions, 2004.

Iceland's Favourite Places. Tampa, FL: TravelVideoStore.com, 2009.

Websites

english.ust.is

This is the English-language version of the website for the Environment Agency of Iceland. Find out information about Iceland's environment and the various parks and reserves in the country.

www.grapevine.is

This is the website for *The Reykjavík Grapevine,* a magazine that lists upcoming events and attractions in Reykjavík and elsewhere in Iceland.

www.icelandreview.com

Visit this site of the magazine *Iceland Review* for daily news from Iceland and information about current affairs, entertainment, and culture.

www.icetourist.is
This is the official website of the Icelandic Tourist Board. The site provides a good overview of the country of Iceland and lists many things to see and do while visiting.

www.inca.is
This website for the Iceland Nature Conservation Association has news and articles about environmental issues and includes many images from around Iceland.

Places to visit

Blue Lagoon, near Reykjavík
Here you can bathe in the milky-blue spa waters, heated by the earth, right next to the Svartsengi geothermal plant.

Eríksstaðir, west Iceland
This is a reconstruction of a Viking farmhouse, built using only the tools that the Vikings would have used. Guides tell the stories of the first settlers.

National Museum, Reykjavík
The displays here give a good overview of Iceland's history and culture.

Nesjavellir Geothermal Plant Visitor Center, southwest Iceland
Here you can see how the geothermal energy system works. If you take the walking trails around the plant, make sure you stick to the marked route! There are hot rivers and steaming vents all around.

Thingvellir National Park, southwest Iceland
This is Iceland's oldest national park, and the site of the original Althing (a congress or parliament). It is now a World Heritage Site.

Topic Tools

You can use these topic tools for your school projects. Trace the map onto a sheet of paper, using the black outline to guide you.

The Icelandic flag is blue with a red cross outlined in white. The three colors represent three of the elements that make up the island: red is for the island's volcanic fires, white is for the snow and ice fields of the island, and blue is for the surrounding ocean. Copy the flag design and then color in your picture. Make sure you use the right colors!

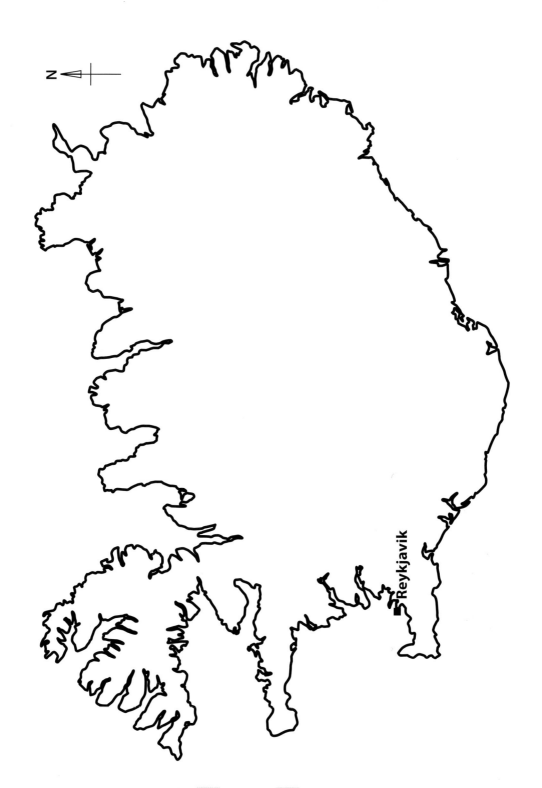

Reykjavik

Index

Titles in the series